RESTORED TO ROYALTY

Living Your Divine Love Story Out Loud

Kellie Surratt

ISBN:9798668328994

Imprint: Independently published

Versions of the Bible used are:

Edited By: Dr. Maxwell Nartey, DHM, NHD

Cover design: Maglara- photo https://www.fiverr.com/dlconcept (layout)

Author's website: www.restoredmovement.net

Printed in the United States of America

DEDICATION

This book is dedicated to every woman who is ready to live the restored life God originally intended for her. No matter your age, nationality, or background, you are loved, valuable, and irreplaceable to the Creator of the Universe! So arise and live your divine love story out loud. The world needs it!

TESTIMONIALS

"Little did I know the plans God had for me when he led me to a women's conference where Kellie was a speaker. My heart knew her immediately as a glory carrier and a God chaser! Was this even possible that such a small young lady was the key to my next? The answer was and is yes! My life has changed forever; I have been blessed to know my Father God in a deeper, more intimate way because of what Kellie has imparted in my life. I am eternally grateful to Kellie for her yes to God, and her yes to mentor me!"

Elder Gwendolyn Hunter
Northfield, New Jersey

"In my darkest moments, Kellie, through the wisdom of the Holy Spirit, almost literally brought me back to life by speaking truth, sharing tools, and shedding light in areas of my life where I needed to come out of hiding. Kellie is a world changer. She listens to the Holy Spirit for His next assignment and then acts in obedience."

Sarah Robbins
Grand Cayman, Cayman Islands

"Kellie is an amazing person who has greatly impacted my life. She invests in my spiritual life; she helps me to embrace my identity of being a beloved daughter of God. She encourages me as I grow in my faith to trust and seek the Lord every day."

Emma Gonzalez
Ciudad Vieja, Guatemala

TABLE OF CONTENTS

Acknowledgements

First and foremost, I express my gratitude to the Lord Jesus Christ; without Him, there would be no book. He is the reason this was able to be penned. It is in Him that I live, move, and have my being. To my mom, thank you so much for teaching me what it means to be resilient and for allowing me to cultivate my gifts and talents; growing up you always found a way to make sure I could dream without limits. To my daddy, I know you are looking down from heaven. Thank you for the tenderness of your heart that no matter my age "daddy's baby, daddy's little girl" is who I was to you, what a privilege to share our journey, your life is making ripples in the earth.

To my godparents Tim and Naomi Smith thank you for saying yes and committing to making an eternal investment in my life when I was fifteen years old, you are part of the village that helped raise this child. To Pastor George Logan, thank you for consistently reflecting Father God's heart and being such a tremendous example of Christ-like character for me. You have a special way of seeing people through the lens of grace and truth, and because of that, I have flourished under your leadership and shepherding. To Dr. Jenny Warren, thank you for looking at a broken college freshman and seeing the beauty and value deep within. To Shonda Hollis, thank you for your realness it peeled back my mask. To the women at New Day Christian Church that took the time to invest in me over the years, thank you. Lastly, to my "tribe" you're scattered around the world, but ladies, you know who you are! Thank you so much for the richness of friendship and sisterhood, each of you adds something unique and special to my life, cheers to journeying together!

Introduction

Royalty has everything to do with identity in Jesus Christ and position as a daughter of The Most High God. There is a divine love story that the Creator of heaven and earth, the God of this universe, the one who eagerly longs to hear you cry out Abba Father, has beautifully woven together for you. Before you ever came into this world, His word says *"all the days ordained for you were written in His book before one of them came to be"* Psalm 139:16 NIV. You are fearfully and wonderfully made, He delights in you and desires for you to awaken to the reality of that delight, of that fierce unrelenting love. He has had you on His heart and in His mind for generations, since before the foundation of the world.

When Jesus was slain it was for YOU, the JOY that was set before Him. He endured and overcame just for you to have the incredible opportunity to be reconciled to the Father, engrafted into His family. We overcome by the blood of the lamb and the word of our testimony. Your divine love story has a voice, a powerful sound, a sound that releases those around you to be restored to royalty. We are a royal priesthood, a holy nation, and a chosen generation!

In October 2003, I had a head on collision with the reality of my divine love story and the One who authored it from before time began, and I have never been the same. My brokenness met with His restoration, my fear with His perfect love, and for that, I'm forever grateful. Will you join me on this journey? For some of you, your divine love story will stir with fresh passion and zeal that will provoke you to action, for some it will awaken a new hunger to return to Your first love, to seek Him again like you once did, and for others of you, your divine love story will be realized for the first time, and you will respond to the One who has been in pursuit of you all along.

2

I believe if you are reading this book, it's because He wants to whisper from His heart to yours, a conversation about your divine love story. My greatest desire for you is that this book ushers you deep into the heart of the most loving father, and that His glorious love captivates you to reckless abandonment of all that you are to all that He is. Through Jesus Christ's finished work may you be restored to the royalty that you are. May you discover more of your true identity, and overflow the purpose and plans of His heart to those around you, because we were made for love.

Amen

CHAPTER ONE

Lost And Found

"But Christ proved God's passionate love for us by dying in our place while we were still lost and ungodly!" Romans 5:8 TPT

I spent my childhood surrounded by family. My next door neighbors for years were my granny and grandpa. If I walked up the dirt road another few hundred feet, then I found myself at my aunt and uncle's house. Summertime was the best with lots of older cousins, aunts, and uncles, fish fries were signature to our weekend agenda. Uncle Marvin would light up the fryer, Motown would blast, card games would start, and lightening bugs would come out. My brother and I would wear out our bikes and skin up our arms and legs doing it! My granny was the best babysitter, back then "Star Search" with Ed McMahon was our show, and double mint gum was our "snack of choice." I would snuggle up with her and my grandpa in their bed as we watched the show. She made the best chicken pie, something about the crust; to this day, I haven't tasted one better!

My father loved to cook and was amazing at it, often we would have holiday gatherings at our house, all piled in the kitchen talking and laughing long after consuming our food. I was my father's shadow when I was a child, I look back at old pictures, and I can truly say I was a daddy's girl all the way! I remember one picture in particular where I was dressed up on Easter Sunday, and I was sitting in my daddy's lap, so proud and so secure. I can't remember a time seeing my parents argue in front of me, which is why I didn't understand why they divorced. I remember thinking, was it something that I did wrong? Was it something that I could help them fix?

My mom, brother, and I moved into an apartment, and daddy stayed at the house. He was hurt, I was hurt, and we both retreated. I retreated out of fear of rejection and fear of abandonment. I knew my daddy as a good father, so I was very confused. Why would a good father no longer be present all the time? It just wasn't fair. Fifth grade was full of stomach problems because of worry and anxiety from all that had transpired.

One weekend I was at my aunt's house, and we were sitting in her kitchen, and I said to her, "I know Jesus loves me, I don't understand it, but I want to be saved." She had often taken me to church with her and her daughters. She asked me if I wanted to wait until Sunday or if I wanted to get saved right then. I wanted to right then, so she called her pastor on the phone, and he led me in a prayer of salvation, that day Jesus became my Savior. It wasn't until many years later that I yielded to His lordship as well (more on that in a later section).

I started middle school extremely insecure; the one thing I felt that I had going for me was that I made the cheerleading squad. Every day I would try my best to dodge my friends when it was time for me to go to my reading remediation class because I was so embarrassed that I struggled to read at the appropriate grade level. As high school approached I decided to try out for the cheerleading squad and made varsity along with another one of my friends. This is just what I needed to "boost" my self-esteem; freshman year of high school offered me the male attention that I craved. I began looking for love in all the wrong places, partying, doing my best to fit in the world's way, but somehow just going through the motions, not really feeling connected to the lifestyle I was participating in.

During high school, my mom, brother, and I joined an awesome church. I began attending the youth ministry where the youth pastor, who would become my godmother, was instructed by the Lord to mentor me, pour into me, and stick it out with me. I was a tough cookie, I remember she asked me to listen to a certain minister who I refused to because I thought she sounded like a man (later she became one of my favorites). I remember her saying that she would reward me for reading a Christian book. I would come to youth ministry after partying, she saw past all of that. I feel like she saw the nine-year-old girl that said, "Jesus loves me, I don't understand it, but I want to be saved."

Thank God for the people that He places in our lives that see us through His eyes and relentlessly pursue us with His love. At this point, I was flirting more with the idea of a life lived in partnership with Jesus. My heart was becoming more sensitive to the things of God, but I was still afraid to fully let Him in. I was afraid He may very well abandon or reject me out of the blue, for seemingly no reason, so it seemed much safer to control my life rather than surrender to His love.

I went to college and spent my first year drinking, partying, being promiscuous, and ultimately almost flunking out. I was so numb from life and unhealed wounds; I was literally at the point of being sick and tired of being sick and tired. I had finally arrived at the end of myself, the place where I could now allow Him to be the potter and me be the clay, October 2003, I got on the wheel. It was fall break my sophomore year of college, and I was in the living room at our house one night and turned the television to TBN (a Christian station), which I never did. As I watched, the lady speaking was sharing her testimony about how the Lord healed her body of cancer, and at that moment, just as clear a person standing in front of me talking, I hear, "just like I healed her body I can restore your soul." I fell to my face lying prostrate on the floor, and I physically felt a heavy blanket of God's love cover me in such a way that I stayed on the floor weeping for a long time. I said to the Lord, "when I was nine years old, I received you as my Savior, but now I want you to be my Lord, I want to live a life surrendered to You, for your purpose."

I got up off the floor, and I called the prayer line that was on the screen and with tears streaming down I said, "I need strength and wisdom to walk out this life with the Lord, please pray for me." I will never forget the sweet soothing voice on the other end as she prayed for me. After I got off the phone with her, I sat on the couch, and I read through the whole book of the Gospel of John. The words on the pages were alive to me, and for the first time I understood what Jesus did was for me. It was personal and intimate; if I had been the only one, He still would have gone to Calvary. That night my life changed forever because I surrendered to mercy filled, grace filled, power filled, glory filled love. I let my Heavenly Father cover me and embrace me like He so desired to all along. I was introduced to the Father heart of God. This started the beautiful journey of Him restoring my soul and leading me in the paths of righteousness for His name sake.

Romans 8:15-16 TPT *And you did not receive the "spirit of religious duty," leading you back into the fear of never being good enough. But you have received the "Spirit of full acceptance," enfolding you into the family of God. And you will never feel orphaned, for as he rises up within us, our spirits join him in saying the words of tender affection, "Beloved Father!" For the Holy Spirit makes God's fatherhood real to us as he whispers into our innermost being, "You are God's beloved child!"*

Reflection

Take time to remember your conversion experience.

When was the first time the Holy Spirit spoke to you?

Who were the people God used to point you to Him?

If you are reading this book and you haven't yet received Jesus Christ as your Lord and Savior, I want to take just a minute to address you. You may have read my testimony and felt something in your heart because you could identify, and just like me, you need your soul to be restored, and you need to be led in the paths of righteousness for His name sake.

John 3:16 TPT says, *"For this is how much God loved the world—he gave his one and only, unique Son as a gift. So now everyone who believes in him will never perish but experience everlasting life.*

Romans 5:8 NLT says, *"But God showed his great love for us by sending Christ to die for us while we were still sinners."*

Romans 10:9-10 NLT says, *"If you openly declare that Jesus is Lord and believe in your heart that God raised him from the dead, you will be saved. 10 For it is by believing in your heart that you are made right with God, and it is by openly declaring your faith that you are saved."*

If this is you and you would like to openly declare that Jesus is Lord, and you believe in your heart that God raised him from the dead, then pray this prayer that you may be saved.

7

Prayer: God, I know that I am a sinner, and there is nothing that I can do to save myself. I confess my total inability to forgive my own sin or to work my way to heaven. At this moment, I confidently rely on Jesus Christ alone as the One who bore my sin when He died on the cross. I believe that He did all that will ever be necessary for me to stand in your holy presence blameless and justified. I thank you that Christ was raised from the dead as a guarantee of my own resurrection. Father God, I ask that you help me to now transfer my trust to Him as His Holy Spirit now dwells in me to lead and guide me into all truth. Thank you for loving me first, I open my heart to receive and accept your love for me. In Jesus name I pray. Amen.

CHAPTER TWO

Personal Restoration: Trading Spaces

"He restores my soul He leads me in the paths of righteousness for His name sake." Psalm 23:3 NKJV

I remember driving home one afternoon, and I had been really, really struggling to let something go. I knew that it was what I was supposed to do, but I just kept picking it back up again in my mind and in my heart. We sometimes think we can fool God by saying things like, "I mean I'm not acting on it", but The Bible says in James 4:17 NLT *Remember, it is sin to know what you ought to do and then don't do it.* I knew that I was to let go of what God asked for fully and completely. That day I was stunned and undone by what the Father spoke to my heart, by His Spirit He simply said, "if you **trust** that I **love** you, then let it go." I began to weep right then and there because what I realized was that He was now tapping into the depths of my soul to begin doing just what He said He could do, which was restore my soul.

In that moment, I realized in order to receive that restoration, I was going to have to trust His love for me in the places of my soul that had been occupied with fear, insecurity, pain, guilt, shame, condemnation, and control. The truth is He was simply saying to me as you trust my love for you, you will let go of what has had your soul (mind, will, and emotions) held captive. That's incredible when we think about the meaning of restore. In the scripture Psalm 23:3, it says He **restores**, indicating that it is continual. So think about the beauty of that! He is continually restoring my soul, bringing me back into the condition of His original intent for my life and leading me into the paths (His ways) of righteousness for His name sake. The Father has an original intent for each of our lives; Christ died and rose again so that we could live out the Father's original intent for our lives as His daughters. We are royalty, fully empowered by Christ's righteousness bestowed upon us not because we earned or deserved it, but because He loves us with no reason attached other than He can't help but be who He is, God is love.

Let's dive deeper into this word "trust". Trust in God in Hebrew is called *bittachon,* which comes from a root word meaning *"to lean on, feel safe, or be confident"[1]*. I think about the activity that many of us are familiar with, the trust fall. One person from the group is chosen to stand on some type of platform that is typically elevated above those who are positioned to catch them. The people that are prepared to catch the person aren't all the same size, and may not be many in number. It could appear as if they may not be strong enough for the person to lean all their weight upon. The person at that point has to decide if they feel safe to fall back, and if they are confident that the people behind them truly have the ability to catch and hold all their weight. The person then takes a deep breath, crosses their arms, and falls back into the arms of those waiting to catch them.

To trust God's love for me, I would have to learn to lean on, feel safe, and be confident in grace and truth. Like the trust fall, I had hands on deck to catch me; only they weren't human hands, they were the "hands" of **grace**, which says in Ephesians 2:8-10 TPT *"For it was only through this wonderful grace that we believed in him. Nothing we did could ever earn this salvation, for it was the gracious gift from God that brought us to Christ! So no one will ever be able to boast, for salvation is never a reward for good works or human striving. We have become his poetry, a re-created people that will fulfill the destiny he has given each of us, for we are joined to Jesus, the Anointed One. Even before we were born, God planned in advance our destiny and the good works we would do to fulfill it!"* And **truth** which says in John 8:31-32 TPT *"Jesus said to those Jews who believed in him, "When you continue to embrace all that*

---

[1] "Bittachon" www.hebrew4christians.com

I teach, you prove that you are my true followers. For if you embrace the truth, it will release more freedom into your lives."

My Mind: Cleaning Out the Clutter

Clutter. What comes to mind when you think of this word? Quite a few things come to mind for me; A cluttered inbox when I have hundreds of emails that need to be deleted, and my closet when I just have too much in it and need to downsize just to name a few. The Merriam-Webster Dictionary defines clutter as, *"to fill or cover with scattered or disordered things that impede movement or reduce effectiveness."*[2] For years my mind had been cluttered with unhealthy thought processes. From childhood I really struggled with fear. The fear was paralyzing, it filled my mind in a way that I truly was distracted from receiving perfect love. 1 John 4:18 NKJV says, *"There is no fear in love; but perfect love casts out fear, because fear involves torment. But he who fears has not been made perfect in love."*

Do you struggle with fear? Are there areas in your life where you can identify that your mind is cluttered with fear, and it's paralyzing you, and distracting you from receiving perfect love? There were three major ways fear manifested in my life causing my mind to be cluttered: fear of death, fear of rejection, and fear of abandonment.

Fear of Death

My mother was pregnant with me when her father died unexpectedly. She was devastated, and it was very traumatic for her. Fast forward some years, I am now seven or eight years old and terrified of death. I was terrified that my mother was going to die; I remember one instance when it was storming outside one day, and my mom was at work. I sat at the window crying until she got home because I was afraid she was going to die in the storm. I would also watch a TV show called "Life goes on" and one of the main characters had AIDS, so I began to be terrified that I was going to get AIDS. I actually ended up in counseling for a short time. My mind would be so filled with fear of death, many times I would think myself sick, or think that I was sick and it was "all in my head." What was the root of this fear for me? Where did it come from? The answer,

---

[2] *Merriam-Webster Dictionary, s.v "Clutter."*

11

from the trauma that my mother experienced when she was carrying me, I know that may sound a little far-fetched for some of you, but stay with me. A few years ago, I went through a brain mapping course for my job as a post adoption social worker. Brain mapping can be defined as *"a technique used to show parts of the brain and how they work together."*[3] It was in the course that I had the "ah-ha" moment regarding the fear of death. I was able to identify what stress and chaos outside the womb affected me in utero.

Though I had not directly battled with the fear of death since my conversion at 19 years old, I discovered that I would subtly and subconsciously battle with it if I heard that someone was sick or injured, if I was sick, if my mom was traveling, or I couldn't reach my dad. I believed the word of God that by Jesus' stripes we are healed, but there was the residue of a root that needed to be cast out. According to Merriam-Webster Dictionary, cast out is defined as, *"to drive out; expel."*[4]

In His perfect love, He was revealing the root to cast out that fear. I was led to a prayer renouncing the spirit of trauma. Where trauma had encroached upon my mind and thinking patterns, I invited His perfect love in to drive out the fear of death that came through the door of in-utero trauma. The Bible says in Ephesians 4:23 NLT *"Instead, let the Spirit renew your thoughts and attitudes.* How does the Spirit change our thinking? It is through the word of God. As I continually feed my mind what the word of God says pertaining to abundant life, I see the victory His love produces in my life and the lives of others.

Fear of Rejection

If we are all being honest at some point or another, we have battled with the fear of rejection. From things like fear of being chosen as last for the team, to fear of being rejected by someone you like of the opposite sex, by a parent when you feel you aren't "measuring up", from a friend when you have a healthy confrontation, and the list goes on. If I'm being honest, I can put a check mark by each of the things that I just listed. Fear of rejection is ugly; it has a way of filling your mind with the

---

[3] "Brain Mapping" https://study.com/academy/lesson/what-is-brain-mapping-test-techniques.html
[4] Ibid., s.v. "Cast Out."

lie that "you are not accepted" which then creates an outward work of striving. Striving to be heard, noticed, liked, and chosen, this was me. The Merriam-Webster Dictionary defines strive as, *"to devote serious effort or energy."*[5] How many of us strive in areas of our lives and can say though I'm putting forth this serious effort and energy it's actually impeding forward movement and reducing effectiveness in my life? That's the lie of rejection, it talks you into "doing more to earn more," earn more love, earn more appreciation, earn more notoriety, and earn more significance.

The opposite of rejection is acceptance, and acceptance speaks a completely different language, especially from the standpoint of our identity in Christ. So let's look deeper into what acceptance means, the Merriam-Webster Dictionary defines acceptance as the following *"the act of accepting something or someone; approval."*[6] These definitions become key as it pertains to our identity in Christ. Because of what He accomplished on the cross, we were granted approval and admittance to be a part of the family of God, no striving on our part, and ANYONE who receives Jesus as their Lord and Savior has access to this acceptance without striving to earn it. It's a free gift, just as I mentioned in the scripture earlier in the chapter, "For it was only through this wonderful grace that we believed in Him. Nothing we did could ever earn this salvation, for it was the gracious gift from God that brought us to Christ!"

Our responsibility is to simply be willing to accept and receive what has been offered to and purchased for us. There is no striving in receiving; many of you reading this book may have been saved for years, but you've been striving to earn what's been accomplished through Christ all because of thought patterns and processes from the fear of rejection that have cluttered your mind and hindered your forward movement in the revelation knowledge of Jesus Christ and His finished work. There is freedom for you, and there is a life of rest. Jesus says in Matthew 11:28-30 TPT *"Are you weary, carrying a heavy burden? Then come to me. I will refresh your life, for I am your oasis. Simply join your life with mine. Learn my ways and you'll discover that I'm gentle,*

---

[5] Ibid., s.v. "Strive."
[6] Ibid., s.v. "Acceptance."

humble, easy to please. You will find refreshment and rest in me. For all that I require of you will be pleasant and easy to bear."

Reflection

In what areas of your life have you been holding on to things that the Lord wants you to release?

In what ways is the Father inviting you to trust His love for you?

In what ways has your mind been cluttered? How is it hindering forward movement in your life or reducing your effectiveness?

Prayer: Heavenly Father, thank you for your perfect love. Thank you that in your perfect love, you have revealed the root of the fear of rejection that has had my mind cluttered, keeping me in bondage to striving. I repent for agreeing with the lies of rejection and acting upon those lies in my life through striving. I ask that by your perfect love, you would now drive out the fear of rejection in Jesus name. As I receive your love, I ask that by your word, you would restore unto me the revelation knowledge of the finished work of Jesus Christ that I may live out of the place of acceptance. I come to the place of refreshing, Lord be my oasis as I join my life with you. Teach me Your ways that I may find refreshment and rest in you in Jesus name. Amen.

Fear of Abandonment

When I think about the word abandonment, the first place my mind goes is a child being abandoned by a parent. I think about the scenarios that create such situations: divorce, imprisonment, irresponsibility, addiction, death, and the list could go on. I fell into the category of divorce; I lived with my mom, and for a long period of time, my father suddenly felt more like a distant stranger (a lot more about that story in the next chapter). The fear of abandonment caused my mind to be cluttered with thought processes and patterns of insecurity that would leak into my relationships. It was nothing for me to project the fact that I was insecure on what someone else didn't do, when in reality, it was false expectations that I had built due to the fear of abandonment. The person was in fact doing nothing to provoke insecurity, but this was the lie that fear of abandonment had created.

How many of us have placed false expectations on people in relationships out of our own insecurities produced by the fear of abandonment? The Cambridge Dictionary defines abandonment as, *"the act of leaving someone or something or of ending or stopping something, usually forever."*[7] The opposite of abandon is stick by. When someone sticks by us, then they never leave us. Our foundational assurance of this is in the Lord. Deuteronomy 31:8 NIV says, *"The LORD himself goes before you and will be with you; he will never leave you nor forsake you. Do not be afraid; do not be discouraged."* When our foundation is built on the assurance that the Lord will never abandon us, no matter what others may do or have done, then we no longer play tug-of-war with insecurity because we are no longer building upon the lies from fear of abandonment.

Reflection

How has the fear of abandonment manifested itself through insecurity in your life and relationships?

Prayer: Heavenly Father, thank you for Your perfect love. Thank you that in Your perfect love, you have revealed the root of the fear of abandonment that has had my mind cluttered, keeping me in bondage to insecurity. I repent for agreeing with the lies of the fear of abandonment and acting upon those lies in my life through insecurity. I ask that by Your perfect love, you would now drive out the fear of abandonment in Jesus name. As I receive Your love, I ask that by Your word, You would restore unto me the revelation knowledge of the finished work of Jesus Christ that I may live out of the place of assurance. Lord, thank you that You go before me, You are with me, and You never leave nor forsake me, help me to not be afraid or discouraged when the temptation arises in Jesus name. Amen.

My Emotions: He Bandages the Wounds

I'm sure many of you have said or heard the phrase "I'm on an emotional roller coaster." If you haven't heard it or said it, I'm sure at some point in your life, you have felt like you are on an emotional roller coaster, you may be feeling as if you are on one in this current season of

---

[7] *Cambridge Dictionary*, s.v. "Abandonment."

your life. Emotions have a way of leading us to places. If I am riding down the street in an Uber on a busy evening in Cairo, and it takes me an hour to get somewhere that usually takes fifteen minutes then impatience can easily lead me to the place of frustration. I find myself being a bit rude to the driver when I exit the car, and it's not even his fault! I then have to regroup and readjust my whole attitude, because my emotions led me to a place.

Let's use an example that's a bit weightier. I keep rehearsing and rehashing the broken heartedness I have experienced because of something that has happened in life circumstantially or relationally. I am now led by emotions of unforgiveness, bitterness, and anger towards myself, God, or others into a place of hardness of heart. I will say both of these scenarios have been my experience, the first one much more recent than the latter, praise God for busy cities ha-ha! Psalm 147:3 NLT says, *"He heals the brokenhearted and bandages their wounds."* I am so grateful for His patience with us. Can I just say that God can handle our emotions when we bring them to Him, He can handle us bringing our entire being to Him. The more that I began to bring Him all of me, the more He was and is able to heal me emotionally. Collins English Dictionary defines a bandage as, *"a long strip of cloth which is wrapped around a wounded part of someone's body to protect or support it."*[8] The Lord Himself protects and supports us when we are wounded; He holds us up and covers us as He heals us.

Many times people are taught to "suck it up", "be tough" or "sweep your emotions under the rug." Then there is the polar opposite where people are encouraged to "express yourself" or "speak your mind" the issue with both is that there is no restorative solution in either if the Lord isn't invited in to heal broken hearts and bandage the wounds. At best, what will end up happening is behavior modification which doesn't produce transformation. It's like having a living room full of furniture and one day you decide to keep the same furniture but rearrange it in the room. The appearance of the room is modified but not transformed because you have the same furniture you've simply changed its placement.

---

[8] *Collins English Dictionary,* s.v. "Bandage."

That's how it is for us when we are led by emotions into a place of hardness of heart; we try to modify our behavior by rearranging the rooms in our heart that are filled with those emotions. Then, we talk ourselves into "being okay" rather than pressing into the One that is ready to do more than make us okay, He is ready to heal us. Psalm 139 1-4 TPT says, *"Lord, you know everything there is to know about me. You perceive every movement of my heart and soul, and you understand my every thought before it even enters my mind. You are so intimately aware of me, Lord. You read my heart like an open book and you know all the words I'm about to speak before I even start a sentence! You know every step I will take before my journey even begins."*

Reflection

What areas of your heart have you hidden from the Lord?

In what areas have you modified your behavior but not experienced true healing?

What areas of your heart have become hardened through life, relationships, or circumstances?

Who do you need to release?

Prayer: Heavenly Father, I come before you first thanking You that through Christ you bring healing to the broken hearted and You bandage their wounds. Father, I repent for allowing emotions to lead me into a place of hardness of heart towards you and others. I ask you to forgive me for harboring unforgiveness, bitterness, anger (and/or anything else you have been harboring that you need to confess and release) in my heart blocking your healing virtue from flowing. I release myself, You, and others (take time to name those who you need to release) from all imprisonment created through my thoughts, words, or actions. You know me deeply and intricately, and because of that, I have complete freedom to be vulnerable and authentic when I approach your throne of grace. Father, I now open up and invite Your healing, I ask You to heal every broken place in my heart and to bind up my wounds as Your word says, and I thank You for it in Jesus name. Amen.

My Will: Learning to Release Control

I think one of the hardest things for us to do is to relinquish control, the reasons may vary but the bottom line is when it comes down to relinquishing what we want, the way we want it, when we want it and how we want it, it is easier said than done most of the time. Learning to release control is a daily process, it's a daily surrender. One of the things that made it so very hard for me to relinquish control when I started this journey with the Lord was the sense of independence. Collins English Dictionary states that *"someone's independence is the fact that they do not rely on other people."*[9] Asking for help has always been a little hard for me. I'm the woman that enjoys helping others, but when it comes to me, my response when offered help tends to sway towards "I'm good, I've got it, thank you though." It's not because I feel that I am above being helped, it's that I truly have learned to do it myself.

When you grow up with a single mom most of your life, and you see her "just do it," you kind of pick up that same ethic. The downside of that is building this complex of doing things in your own strength, and over the years, I had definitely done that. How it played out in my relationship with the Lord is that I would feel like I was a burden to Him, so in the beginning I wouldn't ask Him for help much, I really struggled with it. The truth is, I can only do all things through Christ who strengthens me, not Kellie who strengthens herself. Another way it played out was pride; I had this confidence in my own ability. Many times that manifested by me trying to figure out "how," while telling the Lord the way and when things were going to transpire in my life.

What I didn't realize was that the need to control was creating anxiety, which was ultimately forging a wedge in my intimacy with Lord. It hindered me from deeply knowing Him through experiencing His nature. That's when I began to realize that I needed to understand His goodness. If I really knew experientially that He is good, not just the rehearsed "God is good all the time and all the time God is good" then and only then would I be able to yield to His ways. Why? Because He's good, His guidance is good. The more I experience the nature of His goodness the easier it becomes for me to willingly surrender to His will being done in my life and not my own.

---

[9] Ibid., s.v. "Independence."

18

Reflection

In what areas of your life do you need to rely on the Lord's strength rather than your own?

Do you find it difficult to ask the Lord for help, if so why?

How has clinging to control hindered your intimacy with the Lord?

Prayer: Heavenly Father, I come thanking you that I don't have to do things in my own strength independently of you. I repent for doing things independently of you in my own strength, and I repent for operating in pride and insisting on my own way. I ask that you would begin to give me revelation knowledge of your goodness that I truly yield to your ways and operate in the strength I have through Christ in every area of my life. Father You delight in every detail of my life, help me to cast down arguments and every high thing that exalts itself against the knowledge of God, bringing every thought into captivity to the obedience of Christ when anxiety comes to tell me otherwise. Father, teach me to rest in Your delight, knowing that You always have my best interest at heart in Jesus name. Amen.

The Lordship of Jesus Christ over My Life

When you think of the word Lordship what comes to mind? To some people it may sound a bit intimidating or perhaps domineering. Lexico defines Lordship as, *"supreme power or rule."*[10] John 14:15 NLT says, *"If you love me, obey my commandments."* If we are living our lives under the Lordship of Jesus Christ, then we are living lives obedient and submissive to His commandments. The Bible says in Luke 6:46 NIV, *"Why do you call me, 'Lord, Lord,' and do not do what I say?"*

The words "obedience" and "submission" are like curse words in this generation. To be obedient, somehow implies that your freedom has been stripped, and submission somehow implies weakness. In Christ, it's actually the complete opposite, to be obedient keeps us within the boundaries of our freedom from the sin nature that was blood bought for us by Jesus himself. Every time we obey, we are reinforcing that we are

---

[10] *Lexico*, s.v. "Lordship," https://www.lexico.com.

free from living under the bondage of sin, spiritual death, guilt, shame, and condemnation. We are saying Jesus I love you, and I appreciate what You've done for me, and I want to experience all the abundant life that You have blessed me with has to offer. Once I received this revelation I no longer obey the Lord out of obligation, duty, or unhealthy fear, now it is from a heart posture motivated by love and honor.

The Bible says in James 4:5-7 NLT, *"Do you think the Scriptures have no meaning? They say that God is passionate that the spirit he has placed within us should be faithful to him. And he gives grace generously. As the Scriptures say, "God opposes the proud but gives grace to the humble." So humble yourselves before God. Resist the devil, and he will flee from you."* God, our Father, is passionate in love for us, and when we submit to Him, we are humbling ourselves, receiving His generous grace as well as the ability to resist the devil. I do not believe that we can resist the devil without being submitted to God, it's like a football player going into the game with no helmet or shoulder pads, yikes! I can very clearly remember times that I have not submitted to the Lord and attempted to resist the devil only to find that he wouldn't flee. Submission to God is so important it's like our umbrella of protection against the wiles of the devil.

Reflection

In what ways has your obedience to the Lord been out of obligation rather than love?

How have you viewed the words submission and obedience in your own life?

Prayer: Heavenly Father, I thank you for the gift of Jesus Christ's lordship over my life, and I repent for not always viewing it as a gift. I repent for calling Jesus Lord yet not obeying His commandments and submitting to Him. Jesus, I sincerely desire to know you as my Lord, I say yes to obeying your commands and submitting to you, not out of duty, religion, or merely with my lips, but from a heart posture of surrender to all that You have done for me. Your word says in Philippians 2:13 NLT, *"For God is working in you, giving you the desire and the power to do what pleases him."* Father God, thank you for working in me right now and giving me the power to do what pleases You in Jesus name. Amen.

CHAPTER THREE

Generational Restoration: Gracefully Broken & Beautifully Transformed

"But then I will win her back once again. I will lead her into the desert and speak tenderly to her there." Hosea 2:14 NLT

During my senior year of college, the Lord began to soften my heart towards my father. Even in the midst of the broken promises and cancelled "date days" something was happening on the inside of me. As much as I was disappointed there was transformation happening in the midst of my brokenness. Indeed just as Hosea 2:14 says, the Lord was speaking tenderly to me in the "desert place." As He was restoring my soul, daily I was learning forgiveness is not a feeling but a decision. If I waited until I felt like it to forgive my father, then I may be in the same bitter place today.

The more I chose forgiveness by faith the more I began to take on the Lord's heart for my father. I remember the day the Father said to me, "he may not know how to be your father right now, but you do know how to be a daughter." In that moment, I knew that I was being invited into pressing into my relationship with my earthly father from the position of being a daughter to the Heavenly Father. I would be dishonest if I told you I didn't have to cast down the thoughts of fear of rejection and abandonment in the beginning.

Slowly, my dad and I started talking on the phone more regularly, and I would occasionally go to his house for dinner. I was so happy when he said he was coming to my college graduation, I sensed just how proud he was of me. I was the first on his side of the family among his siblings, nieces and nephews to graduate from a four year university. Shortly after I graduated college, I left to become a missionary in the Cayman Islands on a yearlong assignment. My daddy and I kept in touch as much as we could, he was not smartphone savvy! I will never forget the day that he mailed me a blanket for my birthday that said, "You are loved for the little girl you were, the special woman you are now, and the wonderful daughter you will always be." It somehow reminded me of the blanket of the Father's love that I experienced when I was nineteen years old laying on the living room floor. It was as if in that moment the Heavenly Father was saying the same thing. I was scheduled to go home for Christmas to visit family, and all I wanted was for my daddy to receive salvation. When I was young we went to church sometimes, but there was still a burden in my heart for my father to know Jesus the person, not religion.

At the church that I attended in the Cayman Islands, we were on a fast, and one of the things I prayed for was my daddy's salvation. When I went to visit my family for Christmas two days before I returned to Cayman Islands, I was able to lead my daddy in a prayer of salvation! Our relationship continued to be restored, and we created new memories. One of my favorites was taking him to see Natalie Cole and the Charlotte Symphony when he retired. I was learning to love my daddy unconditionally, with no hidden motive and no reason. I was truly learning to walk in a way that kept no count of the "wrongs," I was hoping the best, believing the best, and choosing to endure.

Fast forward to Father's Day 2017. My daddy and I were sitting in church, and the message was about being a godly father. Immediately the Lord began to minister to my heart and let me know that all the years of brokenness in my relationship with my daddy were because he was void of the Fatherhood of God in his life. After my parents divorced my daddy shut out the Father because he felt abandoned and rejected as a broken family was not his choice. The Lord showed me that daddy didn't have the capacity to give, which is why I had to be his daughter in spite of what he wasn't able to give, because love gives at the expense of self. If me intentionally being his daughter is what was necessary for not only our restoration but his restoration with the Father, then I'm so, so grateful.

That day after church, we went back to my daddy's apartment before going to dinner, and for the first time, I told my daddy that I forgave him for not being the godly father that I needed from nine to twenty-one years old. I told him that I understood now that he too felt rejected and abandoned but that the Father loves him so much and that the bitterness in his heart was not truly who he really is. With tears coming down both of our faces, my daddy said, "I know." We prayed together, and it was one of the most powerful moments that we had together. At that moment, I knew my daddy's capacity to truly receive the Heavenly Father's love was restored. Little did I know it was so vital for the journey that was just ahead as perspective would be everything.

I went to bed one night in August 2017, not knowing that my life was going to be forever changed the next day. I will never forget sensing the presence of the angels of the Lord ministering to me all night, I physically felt overshadowed by the presence of the Lord. All that kept stirring in my spirit is that God is a good, good father. When I woke up, I knew that supernaturally, the Lord was preparing me for something.

I started that day as normal and went to an outreach meeting for ministry, and during that meeting, I received a call from my daddy. He shared that he was in the hospital because he had been in such pain that he could hardly walk. It was as if the moment froze as I heard him say, "Kellie, they think its cancer." I immediately started crying and told him that I was on my way to him. When we got off the phone I cried, and I remember hearing sweetly and softly, "I'm a good, good father." He had prepared my heart the night before, and he had prepared my daddy's heart a few months before on Father's Day because this time during extreme adversity that he did not choose, he would run to the Father's loving arms rather than away from Him.

When I arrived at the hospital, my daddy and I talked. I had him move over, and I cuddled next to him in the hospital bed. I shared with him the encounter that I had with the Father the night before, and at that moment, we both agreed that we were in it together and that we would magnify the Father in His goodness on this journey, no matter what. We both believed for his healing on this side of heaven. We waited until the results came, and the doctor shared that it was stage four Multiple Myeloma and it was in his pelvic area, which affected his walking. My daddy was devastated at the news because he loved walking five miles around the track every day with his friends; he had been doing it for several years. I remember him saying that it was one of the joys in his life.

At that moment, I asked daddy if he would like to learn what it meant for the joy of the Lord to be his strength, he said yes, and we prayed inviting the Lord into the situation. The doctor came in and went over treatment plan options, and daddy chose one. I asked him if I could pray that he wouldn't experience any side effects from the treatment, and he said yes. My father never once had nausea, never lost hair, never was weak, never lost nails after his treatments, and drove himself to each appointment. In fact, for months, he still walked two miles a few times a week with his friends. He would share stories about his nurses and the other patients he was growing fond of during his weekly treatment time.

At some point he told me that he wanted to start journaling his everyday life and title it "My Journey on the King's Highway." He would let me read it, and it was beautiful because I would vicariously get to know my great grandmother Tessie as he weaved things that she had taught him into his daily journey, those memories are what inspired the title of his journal. One day it was in my heart to ask my dad to lay hands on me to pray over my life and my future, I don't recall that he had ever done that before. In my heart, I knew that I would know when it was supposed to happen. One day I was at his apartment reading his journal entries from the previous few days, he had written about me being his inspiration and how proud of me he was. I began to cry, and I knew in my heart, it was the day to ask my daddy to pray over me. As he prayed, I cried, and it was a tender moment because just months ago, I was praying over him and his life. His treatment continued to go well for the next few months, there were a few bumps in the road with flu and pneumonia, but the Lord in His goodness brought him out. His doctor was hopeful for remission, and the x-rays even showed that the lesions were shrinking.

In December of 2018, daddy was not feeling well, so we went to the hospital, his kidney function had declined, and he needed a blood transfusion. We met with his doctor who was shocked to say that the cancer had spread to his shoulder and that the treatment had stopped working. He told us that my daddy's kidneys were failing and that he was sorry, but it looked like weeks. Both daddy and I had to regroup, because we both felt that the wind had been knocked out of us. At that moment, choosing to trust the goodness of the Father became so much more real. We believed for healing, seeing results, and now we faced devastating news.

In January 2019, as things continued to decline with my daddy's health, I remember crying out to the Father for a miracle and earnestly asking Him to extend my daddy's life here on earth. I remember telling the Father how unfair it was that I wouldn't have him walking me down the aisle when I get married and how my kids would never know him. My daddy had been miraculously restored to life before, so why not now? In the middle of my gracefully being broken, it came down to the question, "am I still a good Father no matter what?" It was a moment of transformation, as my answer was "yes, yes, you are still a good father, no matter what." He then stirred my heart with this verse Psalm 22:10 NIV *"From birth I was cast on you; from my mother's womb you have been my God."*

February came, and I remember the day that my daddy and I went out to the store for the last time. I met with my pastor that week and I was a mess, I cried uncontrollably in his office as I told him I knew that it was time to get Hospice involved. I had worked at Hospice as a bereavement counselor for a few years but never imagined being on this side of the fence with one of my parents at thirty-five years old. He looked at me, and he said, "you're it daughter and caregiver, so the question is, are you ready to release your dad?" With tears streaming, I said yes because I had reconciled in my heart that God is a good father no matter what.

My daddy and I had a talk about Hospice home care coming, and I moved in with him to be his 24/7 caregiver. I had the best team, they were all believers, and the Father's goodness overflowed in that. I remember when they brought in my daddy's hospital bed, I was nervous because we were going to have to somehow get him downstairs. My uncle came over that day to help me move him. Daddy said, "give me a minute, I'm going to take one more walk in this earth." My uncle and I watched the Lord supernaturally strengthen my daddy, and without our help, he walked down the flight of stairs and got into his hospital bed. When I got him comfortable in his bed, he said to my uncle, "we army boys always have some strength in reserve," I laughed.

From that time, he would have a month left on this side of heaven. During my daddy's last month, my mom began to visit my daddy, and the Lord beautifully reconciled what was needed between them. I had beautiful conversations about life and memories with both my parents. The first two weeks of caregiving were exhausting yet grace filled. Just a few months before that I had given him the book *Daddy God* by Dr. Jerry Grillo Jr. He read it in a matter of days and I could tell that it ministered to him deeply. One morning after my daddy woke up, I heard him praying the most beautiful prayer to the Father, he asked him for courage for his journey, I sensed Him meet my daddy in that moment. The Father knows what we need and when we need it, and He is always right on time!

At the end of the first two weeks, daddy went to the Hospice house for five days of respite. Let's be honest, he was happy to have a little break from me. I remember him telling my mom "please tell your daughter to stop calling me all the time this is supposed to be our break from each other I'm okay." When mom relayed daddy's message, I laughed and said to myself, "Kellie rest, he's okay." I was in prayer one morning while my daddy was in respite, and I began to sing the song of the Lord over him, a song of love and goodness.

My prayer was that he would have absolute assurance that his journey on the king's highway was destined for heaven, for eternal life, because in Christ there is only victory. I remember the overwhelming feeling of anxiety that I personally battled with, just as I had sang the song of the Lord over my daddy, I needed to hear the song of the Lord over me, and I needed His tender words. He spoke Psalm 62:5 NLT, *"Let all that I am wait quietly before God, for my hope is in him."* It was the moment when the Lord supernaturally quieted my soul with hope in Him. I went into the final two weeks with my daddy having my gaze fixed on the One who my hope is built on, Jesus.

When daddy returned home from respite, the first thing that he told me about was his experience at the mountain of the Lord. He almost couldn't even describe how glorious it was, I said, "daddy were you overwhelmed with his goodness and love?" He replied, "ah man, yes". He said,

"Kellie, I don't know how much longer I will be here, I don't know how much longer I can stay maybe three days." It was three days after his return that he ate his last meal, and his body began to actively shut down. There was a southern gospel station that daddy really enjoyed listening to the last two weeks. One night "Blessed Assurance" came on and daddy started singing it, I joined him in praising our Savior, then we said our goodnight. I asked the Lord to prepare me for each shift in this phase of daddy's transition because I sensed that the Lord wanted it to be full of His glory and that he wanted me to partner with Him in that. The Lord gave me Psalm 32:8 NIV, *"I will instruct you and teach you in the way you should go; I will counsel you with my loving eye on you."*

He had one final thing on his "bucket list" and that was to go sit outside in the fresh air one more time to feel the sunlight. Ten days before he passed away, the Lord nudged my heart, and I knew it was the day for him to go outside one last time. I asked daddy if he wanted to go outside in his wheel chair and he said ok. I got him all bundled up and into the wheel chair, and wheeled him out to the back porch. I will never forget how he enjoyed that and the way he soaked it all up. I took a picture to capture the moment. Physically it was hard for both of us, but in the Father's goodness we were strengthened so that he could give daddy his heart's desire. I told the Father that I was unable to be alone at my daddy's apartment with him when he transitioned to heaven. I really desired for him to be at the Hospice house during his last few days so that he could have the professional care needed. I asked the Father to let me know when my time as the caregiver was completed. I remember walking outside on a Saturday, four days before my daddy transitioned to heaven, and the Lord said to me, "well done, you have been faithful, after today you are released, and I will care for your daddy."

Saturday night was so hard; as my daddy's breathing started changing; he had secretions and sounded like he was gargling water each time he inhaled. I felt so helpless; I stayed up all night with him. He could barely swallow the liquid pain medicine. The next morning I was standing in the kitchen at the window, and spontaneously praise and worship overflowed out of me. I lifted my hands to the Lord and worshipped Him in the beauty of His holiness. I knew a release was happening, and I knew it was time for my daddy to go to the Hospice house for his final few days.

I went over to him with tears flowing yet composed enough to lay my head on his pillow and tell him in his ear how much I loved him, how good of a father he was, and how much he meant to me. Then, I told him that it was time for us to let each other go, he was tired, and it was okay. He mustered up the strength to whisper, "okay, dear." I laid my hand on his head, and I started to pray over my daddy, and the tangible presence of the Lord came into the room in such a heavy way that I had to lie down after praying. Shortly after that, the nurse came, and as soon as I opened the door for her, I burst into tears and told her that I couldn't do it alone from this point on. She was amazing and so comforting; she got him into the Hospice house, in the exact same room where he had experienced the visitation from the Lord!

One of the things that my daddy asked me to promise him is that I would not leave him. He was so happy to hear my voice when I walked into his room two days before he passed away. My aunt said, "he didn't light up like that for us when we walked in." The Father in His goodness let me know the exact day that would be my daddy's last day on earth. The day before that, I went to visit my daddy, and John 11 was on my heart, and I softly heard "this sickness isn't unto death." I felt compelled to read John 11 to my daddy. John 11:25-26 NIV was what the Father was highlighting for my daddy, and it says *Jesus said to her "I am the resurrection and the life. The one who believes in me will live, even though they die; and whoever lives by believing in me will never die. Do you believe this?"* The next night I went to kiss daddy and tell him that I would see him later, that he was finishing out his journey on the King's highway tonight, only to end up in the King's presence.

Reflection

Are there relationships in your life where you love others with conditions?

Are there areas in your life where you need to reconcile that God is good no matter what?

Prayer: Heavenly Father, your love never fails it hopes the best, believes the best and it endures. I ask that you help me to see those around me through your eyes, with Your perspective and Your heart of affection that the conditions that I've put in place may be removed. Father, you are good and though things happen in life that I do not understand, the truth of who You are does not change. Father where unexpected outcomes in my life have blurred my vision from seeing You as good, I ask that you would restore my vision that in every season, be it mountain top, valley low or in between I will see from the lens of Your goodness, in Jesus name. Amen.

CHAPTER FOUR

Living My Divine Love Story Out Loud

"For it is Christ's love that fuels our passion and motivates us, because we are absolutely convinced that he has given his life for all of us. This means all died with him, so that those who live should no longer live self-absorbed lives but lives that are poured out for him—the one who died for us and now lives again. So then, from now on, we have a new perspective that refuses to evaluate people merely by their outward appearances. For that's how we once viewed the Anointed One, but no longer do we see him with limited human insight." 2 Corinthians 5:14-16 TPT

Christ's Love is My Fuel

Often we see the expression "live out loud" manifested in our society, and most of the time it's associated with worldly living. What does it mean for us as believers to live out loud? I believe Apostle Paul summed it up so beautifully in 2 Corinthians 5:14 TPT when he said, *"For it is Christ's love that fuels our passion and motivates us, because we are absolutely convinced that He has given His life for us all."* How powerful this verse is, to have a life that is fueled by Christ's love. What happens when Christ's love is the driving force in our lives? We begin to live out loud! When I encountered the Lord at nineteen years old, and He completely wrecked my world, I began to see other people through different lenses. I remember one of the first books that I read was *Good Morning Holy Spirit* by Benny Hinn. I can remember being in my room while reading that book and saying to Lord all I want is for you to use my life for your glory. I didn't make a special request as to how, but I just made myself available.

I returned to college after fall break my sophomore year, and was on fire for the Lord! I would soon start a women's bible study/fellowship group in my dorm, was singing on the praise team, and had a hunger for the Word of God. As my priorities had shifted so did my grades, I made the dean's list, and my GPA increased significantly. I remember being home from school one weekend, and my pastor's wife asked, "what happened to you?" that's how drastic the transformation was! What happened to me was the glorious love of Jesus! As a young teenager, one of the things that I was into was modeling. After becoming a laid down lover of Jesus, what was once solely a vanity thing in my life became a tool for me to share His love with others.

During my senior year of college I was in the Miss North Carolina USA Pageant. My heart posture was so different from before, I wasn't in the pageant with the hope of winning, I was in it with the hope of sharing Jesus. The night of the competition, before we all went out, it was on my heart to gather the contestants so we could pray over the night and over the one who would be crowned Miss North Carolina USA. I led us in prayer, it was powerful, at the end of the prayer another girl led singing "Amazing Grace" we all joined in and sang, and truly the focus, the why behind the night shifted in that moment. That year Miss North Carolina went on to win Miss USA.

As my major in college was human services, I wanted to embark on an internship that would bring a mix of counseling and social work. The door opened for me to intern as a crisis pregnancy counselor, I loved it so much, and I loved the girls that I counseled so much. It was a Christian organization, which gave me the opportunity to share the gospel and pray with the girls. Christ's love was compelling me, and I was truly beginning to regard others not merely by their outer appearance but through the Lord's eyes. Christ's compassion, His mercy was coming alive in my heart in such a way that I just wanted to spend my life sharing Him with others; "yes, I will go" is what stirred in my heart!

Those four words said from a willing and obedient heart, and a made-up mind changed my life! I came to the Lord not knowing where "yes I will go" would lead just knowing that I was finally ready to find out. So the journey began and I went...to the young women on my campus... to the pregnancy crisis center.... to the homeless man on the street... to the prisons...to schools...to the teenage girls attempting and contemplating suicide... to the park where high school kids hung out during lunch... to the broken woman in the Wal-Mart parking lot... to the depressed woman in the line of Sam's Club... to the woman who could not afford her groceries... to the neighbors...to the nursing home...to the sweet old lady in the hospital...to the discouraged makeup artist...to the grieving...to the dying...to the drug dealers...to the prostitute...to the girls home. He was leading me to the one, leading me to leave the ninety-nine, the crowd, and go after the one on an everyday basis, as a lifestyle. He was teaching me to daily live out loud fueled by His love, motivated by it, and seeing others through it, because One died for all.

I had no agenda when I asked Him to use me for His glory; I wasn't envisioning a grandiose platform just a life poured out. Because of the experience of what He had done for me, I yearned for others to experience the same powerful love. It was almost the end of my senior year, and I had no concrete plans regarding what I was going to do once I graduated. I remember so clearly saying to the Lord, "Lord I was serious when I surrendered my life to you, and Your plan for me, I have no plan so what is Your plan once I graduate?" I remember sitting with my pastor and his wife at their home shortly before graduation, and they asked me what my plans were. I said jokingly, so I thought, "I think I'll go work with youth on an Island somewhere." Little did I know what I spoke was the Lord's plan.

I Am a Minister of Reconciliation

"Now, if anyone is enfolded into Christ, he has become an entirely new creation. All that is related to the old order has vanished. Behold, everything is fresh and new. And God has made all things new, and reconciled us to himself, and given us the ministry of reconciling others to God." 2 Corinthians 5:17-18 TPT

How beautiful are these verses, we are entirely new creations in Christ, EVERYTHING fresh and new. This is the incredible power of the gospel of Jesus Christ; this is what love did, He made ALL THINGS NEW in

Him, wow! Because we have been made new and have been reconciled to God, the scripture says He, not man has given us the ministry of reconciling others to God. Wait, this means that ALL true believers have a responsibility to reconcile others to God, it's not just the preacher, apostle, prophet, evangelist, pastor, and teachers! The King James Dictionary defines reconcile as, *"to conciliate anew; to call back into union and friendship the affections which have been alienated; to restore to friendship or favor after estrangement."*[11]

I graduated from college, and upon graduation, I had come to know the plans of His heart for me. I was to go and be a minister of reconciliation in the Cayman Islands with Youth for Christ as a Youth and Community Worker for a season, reconciling children and youth to Father God, through the fuel of the love of Jesus. I had never been outside of America, other than Mexico for a month of study abroad during my senior year of college. One night I read Genesis 12:1 NLT *"The LORD had said to Abram, Leave your native country, your relatives, and your father's family, and go to the land that I will show you."* It was as if the Lord said, "Kellie leave your native country, your relatives and your father's family and go to the land that I show you." It was then that I knew this was the Lord's invitation to come away with Him. I knew that Cayman Islands would only be the beginning of leaving my native country. I talked with my parents, and my pastor, and everyone blessed me to go and be a minister of reconciliation. I spent a year in Grand Cayman Island, and God did beautiful and wonderful things in and through me.

I am an Ambassador of Christ

"We are ambassadors of the Anointed One who carry the message of Christ to the world, as though God were tenderly pleading with them directly through our lips. So we tenderly plead with you on Christ's behalf, "Turn back to God and be reconciled to him." For God made the only one who did not know sin to become sin for us, so that we who did not know righteousness might become the righteousness of God through our union with him." 2 Corinthians 5:20-21 TPT

The International Standard Bible Encyclopedia defines an Ambassador as *"an official representative of a king or government."*[12] I remember

---

[11] *King James Dictionary,* s.v. "Reconcile."

once being in a meeting with a very high ranking government official from a particular nation. The president at that time had arranged for the meeting to take place. I will never forget what happened in the meeting that day. As we were talking the Spirit of the Lord began to invade the place and I shared with this governmental official that I had been praying for the nation for many years and she shared with me that she knew that our meeting was God ordained because she and her father began to intercede for the nation during the same year. We continued talking and out of my mouth came the words "I'm in this nation as an ambassador." I began to pray and prophesy over the government official, and the Lord absolutely met us in a special way in that moment. I believe with all my heart in that moment that He was reminding her that she too is an ambassador, here to represent the government of the kingdom of heaven in the government of the earth.

As daughters of the Most High God, we are now robed in Christ's righteousness, as partakers of His divine nature. This new life that we have is now hidden in Christ; we really do stand as His representatives wherever He calls us to go. The main cry of my heart for the past several years has been, "Lord take me wherever our intimacy leads." It simply means this; I want to go wherever knowing You through experience takes me. It's my "dangerous prayer," the one that always shatters the limits that I can be tempted to put on God. It's the prayer that always brings me back to my knees in hunger for more of Him. It's the prayer that keeps me humble before Him when He grants me favor in high places. It's the prayer that leads me to partner with Him in carrying the burden of His heart in intercession for certain nations and people groups. It's the prayer that causes me to give Him a new "yes Lord" with every invitation, and it's the prayer that keeps me anchored in living a life of abiding rather than striving.

As His ambassador and minister of reconciliation, I have had the honor and privilege of sharing the gospel of Jesus Christ, the very essence of my divine love story in nations around the world. As I write this book, I am currently sitting in my room at my desk in North Africa. Never could I have imagined that my life would be so full of incredible adventure. Though I have been so blessed thus far in my journey, I believe that the latter shall be greater and that I am just beginning! The last two chapters

---

[12] *International Standard Bible Encyclopedia*, s.v. "Ambassador."

of this book are a compilation of stories, testimonies, and excerpts from my journals as I have journeyed around the world. May you be blessed, inspired, stirred, impacted, and motivated to action by what you read. You dear one are His ambassador and minister of reconciliation, and it's time for you to infuse your sphere of influence with your divine love story because you have been restored to royalty.

Reflection

Are you fueled by Christ's love?

How is God inviting you to be a minister of reconciliation and ambassador for Christ in your sphere of influence?

What is your dangerous prayer?

Would those around you say that there is evidence that you live your divine love story out loud?

Prayer: Heavenly Father, may the love of Jesus Christ be the fuel and motivating factor in all that I do. You said in Your word that the love of God has been shed abroad in my heart by the Holy Spirit. I ask you to awaken my soul to the depths of this great love. Father, I ask for boldness to joyfully respond when you invite me to partner with you as Your minister of reconciliation and ambassador of Christ in my sphere of influence. Father, stir my heart with the "dangerous prayer", the prayer that keeps me walking on the water with my eyes fixed on you, the one that takes all the limits off of how you use my life for Your glory. May the evidence of Your inward working in my life produce much fruit through my life in Jesus name. Amen.

CHAPTER FIVE

Acts of Love

"Your lives light up the world. Let others see your light from a distance, for how can you hide a city that stands on a hilltop? And who would light a lamp and then hide it in an obscure place? Instead, it's placed where everyone in the house can benefit from its light. So don't hide your light! Let it shine brightly before others, so that the commendable things you do will shine as light upon them, and then they will give their praise to your Father in heaven." Matthew 5:14-16 TPT

There is beauty in the everyday opportunities to be a part of other people's divine love story. There is also beauty in everyday life lessons we continually learn as we journey deeper into our divine love story. Often we are waiting for a "main event" when in reality, every day that we wake up, the main event has just begun. You may be the only representation of Jesus someone ever encounters. Daily destiny is our portion, and nothing is wasted in the Lord. Your light shining will radiate and reflect the very nature of the Light of the World within you, so wherever you find yourself in the world shine on, shine on!

It's a Family Affair

One of my favorite things when I'm on the field is to have my mom join me for a week. What I love about her time with me is that she comes so ready to serve and be a part of what God is doing through the ministry. My mom and aunt came down to Guatemala for a week, we were so happy to have them. They raised money for stoves to be installed at the homes of some of the beautiful families that we serve alongside two of our dear friends in their ministry to mothers. Not only did they raise the funds for the stoves, but we all went to each house and installed the stoves together. My mom and aunt spent time loving on the families and praying with them. I thank God that it could be a family affair, what a blessing!

Your Feet Are Beautiful

After a somewhat long walk and hike up a steep hill, we arrived at the house of a widow whose home overlooks the entire city of Xenacoj, Guatemala. When we arrived, the precious woman welcomed us and shared her story with us. Her previous home had been flooded, and her granddaughters had taken her in. As I listened to this woman tell us her story, the Lord kept saying "her feet are beautiful." After someone from the group read scripture to the woman, they asked who wanted to pray for her. I immediately felt that I was to pray for her, and we all laid hands on her, and I began to pray. After we prayed, I asked the translator to tell her that her feet are beautiful and that every step she takes the Lord is with her. She shared that sometimes she does not have the strength to walk up the hill. It was strong on my heart to wash and pray over her feet. I and two other girls kneeled down and washed her feet and prayed over them, believing the Lord would strengthen them so that she could continue taking steps...with Him right by her side...because her feet are beautiful.

See Her with My Eyes

The Lord has caused me to become undone because of her presence in my life. She is one of those people that He used to forever change the way I see. When she came to the door the first time, I will never forget how incredibly rundown she looked from head to toe and how mentally oppressed she was. Her clothes were a mess, her skin so filthy, her feet bare, her hair full of lice and lice eggs. At that moment, I had a choice to make, either I see her or I don't. I had an overwhelming impression, supernatural to be honest, and as I saw her in that moment, I went in and talked with the team, and the ladies were in total agreement that we needed to respond to seeing her. Right away, we organized a plan; someone was designated to cook her meal, and someone was designated to get her a toothbrush, clean clothes and shoes out of our abundant supply in the garage.

We had a spare shower in our bathroom in the office, so I brought her in showed her the clothes, and the food that was being prepared for her. Then, she went and took a shower and brushed her teeth for the first time in who knows how long. Once she came out of the bathroom, it was on my heart to clean out the wounds on her feet. So I put on some gloves and cleaned out the wounds. She told me how old she was and that she had children. However, she had been separated from them. She went into the kitchen and ate all that she wanted. She kept saying, "Thank you." I kept looking at her hair and all the lice and lice eggs, and I just remember thinking I see her, and I will respond. So I did a mayonnaise treatment on her hair and combed hundreds of lice and lice eggs out of her hair, there were so many we had to burn the bags I put them in. We prayed the word of God over her, and later that evening she left.

Over the next few months she would come back almost weekly. Our base was in a gated community, so the neighbors were not fond of her coming into the neighborhood, but slowly some of them began to show her love and kindness. She would often ask for me when she came to the door, requesting food, clothes, shoes, or coffee. I would come and join her some days at the entrance of our courtyard; I would share about Jesus sometimes, other times she would just want to sit with me in silence or remind me that she wanted to live with us. A few months after I had returned to America, I received a video from the team, and it was her! She was at the base, and she looked so good. She had heard that they were no longer going to be at that location and wanted to come to say thank you. She told the team that she continued to return to our base because it was the only place where she felt peace. I was in tears because of her message, she simply said, "thank you for taking care of me."

Extreme Makeover: Home Edition

So this past week, I totally felt like my team and I were part of Todd's crew from Extreme Makeover: Home Edition. This month we have the privilege of ministering to Mayan widows and orphans in the city of Santo Domingo Xenacoj, where 90% of the population is Mayan. One of our first ministry projects was to go to a village and tear down the remains of a widow's home so that another team could rebuild a more durable one for her and her children. Upon arrival, our ministry contact shared his heart for his people and shed tears as he told us how poorly widows are treated. Our other contact said, "you can never give them too many hugs." We prayed for the widow, her family, and the village and hugged her before diving in.

She was so grateful and smiled a lot with excitement and anticipation for the completion of her new home. She shared that her husband had died eight years ago from diabetes. As we tore down her old home that was made of bamboo, I encountered big spiders and disgusting centipedes that I typically would have freaked out about and called it quits. I got over myself and my fears in those moments because it wasn't about me AT ALL. There were two little boys from the village that watched us for the longest time and then came and helped. They worked so hard as if it were their home. At the end of the day, the team and I walked away having completed a job well done, selflessly and purposefully.

Answered Prayer

Before I left for Belize, I collected women and children's clothes. All the clothes were very specific sizes, which I was concerned about because I wanted a variety for multiple women and children. I went to Esther's house to deliver clothes to her and her family. I talked with Esther and met her children. When I told her that the Lord wanted to bless her with clothing, and I began presenting the clothes to her, she started crying. She explained that she had been praying for clothes for her and her children so that they could go to church, and this was God answering her prayers. He is absolutely in the details, down to the very size we need. I was so thankful that though I wanted variety, the Father wanted her to have an abundant supply!

Mayan Queens

This month I have the privilege of being in the midst of some of the most beautiful old women I have ever seen. Every wrinkle, strand of hair, article of clothing, and word spoken in Kaqchikel make up the very essence of these "Mayan Queens." The widows of Xenacoj, Guatemala, make my heart glad. They are women of poise, quiet inner strength, perseverance, and grace. It's been so wonderful to pray for them, their families and their villages, and to see a need and meet it, whether it is a hug, a listening ear, or a laugh. One of my teammates and I spent some time with three very special ladies ages seventy, seventy-two, and eighty-two years old. I think they laughed with and at us more that night than they had in a long time. My teammate washed the eldest ladies' feet, and I gave one of the other ladies some new shoes and the other some earrings, and I painted her nails for the first time in her life! That night I was reminded that these precious women are the Lord's Mayan Queens.

Labor of Love

In the heat of the Philippines, we had at least fifty twenty pound bags to haul up the hill from the bottom of the riverbank. This cement would be the only thing that would cause the foundation of this family's house to be secure in a storm. They were so grateful to see our team there. I looked at the hill, and all the bags of cement, and I didn't know if I could do it. I put myself in their shoes for a moment and quickly decided yes, I can do it. With each bag, I carried up the hill, I counted down. My legs and arms were shaking, and I felt so tired. I fell on my face, headed back down the hill in one of my many trips, and had to dig my hands into the ground to keep me from rolling. I wanted to quit, but in that moment, I just reminded myself that they were worth it. When we finished, the family was nearly in tears because they would no longer have to worry about losing their home.

Refuge for Refugees

My heart for these special ones is just so full. Here in Egypt, I have the beauty of Eritrea, Ethiopia, Somalia, Sudan, and South Sudan in my English classes. They all have a story of pain and resilience. A melting pot of Muslims and Christians from fourteen to twenty-one years old is in my midst. I feel like I have seventy-five kids, the way we connect is undeniably the Lord. Our normal day looks like teenage girls with their babies in class with us, and two assistants translating because I have at least two languages in my classes. Somehow it comes together, and these kiddos are rocking with their conversational English. My favorite student in my first semester is a precious Muslim girl from Somalia; she wears a complete covering all I can see are her eyes, but those eyes tell a story. Every class, I praise her for how well she is doing, as she is shy and soft spoken. We often greet one other with a hug and kiss on the cheeks. My heart is to communicate love in a way that they truly feel it, as my classroom is a refuge for these precious refugees.

Treasures in the Dumpster

Today was one of the hardest and most beautiful days of ministry that I have ever experienced. Today our squad went to the largest dumpster in Honduras and fed two hundred people. I was overwhelmed with emotion when we arrived. About two hundred and fifty families live in and call the dumpster home. They share living quarters with vultures, dogs, cows, and thousands of pounds of trash. Shortly after we arrived, a lady named Luz who lives in the dumpster, walked up and hugged me. She shared that she has breast cancer, immediately some of us prayed for her healing. After we prayed, she shared that she also had knots in her stomach, I laid my hand on her stomach to feel them, and they were quarter to golf ball size.

One of my squad mates prayed that the knots would no longer exist, as I had my hand on the knots. Luz and I continued to have conversation after we prayed. I asked her if she was in pain before we prayed for her, and she said yes, but that after we prayed, she felt better. I then met a man named Franklin who has been living in the dumpster for two years, he shared that he has two children and that tomorrow is the birthday of one of them. He shared that he wished that he could get presents. At that moment, I had the opportunity to share with him that his love for his children will always be a greater gift than any material thing. I was then able to talk with him about God's love and pray with him. I met Fannie, Alexandria, and Catelina too, all precious, joyful, and full of gratitude. Today I learned that the Father has beautiful and valuable treasures even in dumpsters.

His Hands and Feet

We sounded the alarm for all the prayer warriors to intercede with us as we were in the Philippines, and Super Typhoon Yolanda was expected to hit. We had teams on a few different Islands and we believed that the Typhoon would turn and not hit the Islands as projected. To God be the glory the Islands we were on at most, experienced light rain showers. The squad was eager to head to other locations to help where the Typhoon had hit. We were able to send a team to help on the ground, while a few of us collected items to give to a family that had been affected by the Typhoon.

41

The team came back with such heart wrenching stories. One, in particular, stands out at the forefront of my mind. One of the girls shared that she aided a man who had lost his entire family. He had climbed to the top of a tree with his children in his arms to try to escape the water. As he told her this story, he was alone as his children died in his arms in that tree. Seeing the suffering can be so overwhelming at times, but also so glorious because we are the light of the world, we possess the very hope that is needed in these times. We really are His hands and feet carrying and distributing His powerful love in this World. We are the difference because He is the difference.

Born on Purpose

Let me just be completely honest right now, God rocked my world and flooded my heart with a love I can say I've never felt before. My team and I started the morning at 4am to travel about three hours from where we were in Honduras to the ministry that we would be serving at for the day. We were all super excited because we would be working with teenage mothers who had been victims of rape and/or incest and their babies. Upon arrival, we were greeted by the ministry founder who, by the way, is totally an Angelina Jolie in the movie Salt, only for the kingdom of God. She is an amazing woman of God who absolutely trusts Him 100% with her life. She not only cares for the teenage girls and their babies, she also has a victim ministry and rescues women and children from all types of violence. To date, she has helped about four thousand victims. She shared with us that her daughter was conceived through rape twenty-six years ago.

She had so many courageous stories; she is definitely a modern day Esther. After a brief orientation, she introduced us to the mothers, their babies, the staff, and gave us a tour of the property. Immediately I was drawn to this precious little two-year-old boy who, to me, was the most beautiful thing I'd ever seen. He immediately came to me smiling, and I picked him up, and he just embraced me. After holding him for a few minutes, I felt strongly in my heart that I was to pray over him, so I asked if it was okay, and right before I began to pray, the Holy Spirit ministered to my heart that I was to pray for him like a mother would her child.

I prayed for his life his past, present, and future, and in that moment, love welled up in me like I have never experienced before. I spent most of my time that day playing with and loving on this little guy. Now that you know what was stirring in my heart, let me share with you his story, which initiated it all. This precious little guy was conceived through incest; his mother got pregnant by her father. About a year ago, his mother who is under eighteen years old, abandoned him and planned to sell him so that she could live on her own means. He may have been conceived through incest, but he was born on PURPOSE. I know that God has an awesome plan for his life and I'm so grateful that He used me to be one of the vessels that declare that over him. Until yesterday, I never knew what love at first sight was all about. I can only imagine the Father looking at us at first sight and saying, "how you got here may not make sense, or may have been an injustice, but I love you, and YOU were born on purpose!"

The Language is Love

I had so many thoughts about what the upcoming months ahead in Europe would look like, particularly how I would be able to reach people and communicate with them through the language barriers that were inevitable. In Central America, I was able to speak and understand Spanish well enough to connect with people and build relationships. For the first time, I was faced with the feeling of inadequacy and really wondering what kind of impact I would have with people in the months ahead. When we arrived in Albania, and I heard people speaking in Albanian, it was even more intimidating because the language sounded very hard to learn. We went into town the first weekend we were here, and after purchasing pastries, a few of us sat in a small park area, and there was a cute old lady sitting on the bench across from us crocheting.

I looked at her and waved, and she waved back, I was so excited! I really wanted to go and talk with her, and after contemplating it for a little while, I did. When I walked over and sat down, she showed me the bootie she had made and started talking to me in Albanian, though I didn't understand a thing, I just kept smiling and communicating with body language. After a few minutes, I showed her my camera on my phone and asked in the best way that I could if we could take a picture and she said yes! We took the picture, and I showed it to her, and she laughed and patted my cheek. Later in the afternoon as we were walking back to our home, I saw the sweet lady passing by on the bus, we locked eyes, she smiled, and we waved goodbye to one another.

As the month has progressed, I've had fun interacting with the people that surround me from the ladies who cook for us, to the local vet that comes to the property, to our ministry host, and my most favorite, his house keeper. I've even managed to pick up a few words in Albanian! Culturally people don't typically hug unless they are close or related. The housekeeper here speaks a little English, and as she and I began spending more time around one another, she shared that when she welcomed us to the property she knew I was there for her. We have spent many days since making coffee for the squad in the mornings and talking about our lives, I am getting the best hugs and kisses on the cheek from her. I have realized that whether I know the language or not His love will always be able to communicate itself through me.

Abuelita (Grandma)

It never fails that I adopt a new family member in other nations. This one though, it feels like we are cut from the same cloth. When my mom and aunt visited I took them to meet Abuelita Maria. I will never forget when they walked into her house, they were shocked and said, "oh my gosh, this is Grandma Ida, Grandma Ida has a twin." Grandma Ida was my great grandmother who I never got the chance to meet. Mom sent me a picture of Grandma Ida once she returned home, and they truly do look like twins, I was amazed.

She has our picture on her dresser where she can see it every day. She's the eldest beauty in mom's ministry, she is our matriarch, little in stature but big in presence. She was widowed for many years. She told me the story of her and her husband and how she called herself Carmelita because he liked it, she would giggle as she told me and from time to time I would call her Carmelita and she would laugh and say "no, no." I was blessed to be able to help take care of her basic needs; it was the Lord's way of reminding her that He sees her and that she wasn't forgotten. One of my favorite things was for her to come to the grocery store with us to pick out what she wanted. She got to try new things that she really liked, and she was so excited about it. Her heart of gratitude is so tender and sincere.

Welcome to the World Baby Girl

Never did I imagine that I would be able to say I helped support mothers as they delivered their babies in Mbarara, Uganda! As the day started, we headed to the hospital in full anticipation of an eventful day. I arrived at the maternity ward; to my left was a room full of women who had just had their babies. It was so full, there were mattresses with women and their babies lined up on the floor. Just down the hall, a short distance on the left was the delivery room.

As we walked in, we were welcomed by the midwives, medical students, and doctors. The room was small and had three beds for delivery. Each bed was only separated by a curtain and about three feet of space. I was shown where to wash my hands and then given gloves. Before I knew it, all three beds were full of women who were ten centimeters dilated and ready to push!

There was one particular woman that was very vocal, it was her first baby, and she was scared. I went over to her and began to rub her back and do some breathing exercises with her. After a few minutes, I asked her if I could pray for her, and she smiled and said yes. So I prayed for a smooth delivery and peace over her as she labored. Just minutes after that, she felt the urge to push, and in no time, the baby was born.

Within about thirty minutes after the baby was born, her mother was stitched and cleaned up. She thanked me for praying for her, put her clothes on, stood up, gave me two thumbs up, and before she walked out to the post delivery room said with a big smile, "alright I'm good now" like childbirth was a piece of cake...umm WOW! Later I went to see her and the baby, we laughed and talked about life, and I held the sweet bundle of joy. She shared that she is a Christian, and when I asked to pray for her, she was so happy because it refocused her to call on Jesus to help her during the delivery. I absolutely saw His grace and hand in that delivery today, as if He was sweetly saying, "welcome to the world baby girl."

He Cleans Off the Dirt

If you would have asked me a few days ago if I thought I would be in the middle of a very dark and oppressive Gyspy ghetto in Sandanski, Bulgaria cleaning children's filthy, snot covered face with baby wipes loving every moment of it because Jesus was speaking to me through it I would have said NO! This was my favorite part of my day on Wednesday, May 8th. As we went outside at 10 am in the morning, we were greeted by the sound of music playing in the streets. As we started to sing kids from all over the neighborhood began to gravitate to us. Within just a few minutes, there were kids everywhere.

As I looked around at the children, I saw many faces that were hiding under layers of dirt. So I decided to go to the store and get baby wipes so that I could spend time cleaning the faces of the children. One at a time, I called them over and tried my best to explain that I was going to wash their face. As I washed their faces, I smiled and told them how beautiful they were, they smiled back and gladly cooperated while I removed the dirt and crust from their faces. Some faces were dirtier than others, but that didn't matter to me because they were worth cleaning. As I was wiping their faces, the Lord reminded me that He does the very same thing for us. He gently calls us to Himself and cleanses the layers of dirt with the purity of who He is. Regardless of the amount of dirt, He is still willing to cleanse us and give us beauty for ashes.

Standing in the Gap

We walked into the church where at least ten thousand people were killed during the genocide in Rwanda. It left me speechless as the tour guide showed us the stains on the walls from the residue of children's brains as they were tossed against the walls. The church was cold; it felt like the genocide had just happened. The tour guide was almost like a zombie when she was taking us through the church. At the end of the tour she shared that she lost her family in the genocide, she watched them take her parents and she managed to get away before they captured her.

I asked her why she chose to work there and relive the pain of that trauma over and over again each day. She shared that it was the only job she was able to get. Feeling the weight of her oppression, I asked her if I could pray for her she said yes. As I prayed those who were with me from the team laid hands on her, I could feel the weight of her burden, and at the same time, I could feel the help of the Lord intervening on her behalf. I hugged her, and though it was a heavy day if the only reason that I was truly at the memorial site was to stand in the gap for her, then it was absolutely worth it.

Choosing Love

It's hot in Rwanda, and we are about sixteen girls to one house right now, and about five girls piled in one room. I am sharing a bed with one of the girls that, quite honestly, I am learning to love well. So I wrote her a letter today and told her I haven't always loved her well, but I so desire to, and I'm learning. I'm intentionally going to spend time with her because I want to see her the way the Father does, not regarding her by the flesh. We have very different personalities, but I want to learn to celebrate our differences, not tolerate them. Choosing love isn't easy because it's so much weightier than lip service to people, love is an action word. If I say it and people don't experience it and can't see it, then that's simply flattery, not love.

CHAPTER SIX

Demonstrations of Power

"For the Kingdom of God is not just a lot of talk; it is living by God's power." 1 Corinthians 4:20 NLT

I love this verse, because it heralds the truth that we serve a living God, a resurrected Jesus Christ who is fully active, the same yesterday, today and forever more. When we live our lives believing and embracing this then we become proof providers that He who says it will perform it. What a privilege that we have to partner with the Holy Spirit to glorify Jesus in the earth! When the power of God is demonstrated it reveals His love, zeal and passion. Healing is for today, miracles are for today, and deliverance is for today!

He Hears

We went through security, got patted down, and then had our hand stamped. At the entry way of the prison there were buckets of food with flies in it, I thought to myself, "this food is not for human consumption." As we walked through the corridors I saw women with their young babies, I was in shock. Soon we arrived at the group of women that we would minister to. It was such a diverse group each woman shared a bit of their story and why they were in prison.

Stories ranged from drug charges, to theft, to attempted murder. After the women shared their stories, I was overwhelmed by the presence of the Father and His love. I had interceded for the women in prison in Guatemala before I ever moved there, and in that moment, I knew that I was sitting in the presence of some of the very women I had interceded for. I began to tell the women how much the Father loves them. I also shared that in 2011, I started interceding for Guatemala, and during that time, I prayed for women in prison.

One of the women spoke up and said, "I was one of the women you were praying for in 2011," I got saved then, crying she said, "thank you I received Jesus because of your prayers." Another woman spoke up crying and said, "last night I just asked God to send someone to tell me that He loves me so that I would know that he really does and today He sent you." My dear friend shared what was on her heart, and one of the ladies spoke up and said, "I have dreamt of you two, and you shared this exact scripture in the dream." Another one of the women spoke up and said, "no one ever comes to see us and shares Jesus with us, thank you."

We prayed together and embraced one another and were wrapping up our time when one of the other inmates came over to join us. This woman was full of the fire of God, when she opened her mouth to pray it was overwhelming. She began to prophesy over some of the women, and she began to prophesy over me. I was later informed that she was framed by her sister and was falsely accused of burning down her own house with her husband and son inside. She was sharing a cell with her sister that accused her; she had forgiven her and embraced her time in prison as an assignment from the Lord. She was such bright light in darkness; I will never forget her presence.

Garbage City Greatness

I was so excited to minister in Garbage City, a part of Cairo, Egypt. There was a particularly large number of young men, many fresh off the street and addicted to drugs, exactly what I asked the Lord for! I started ministering at 8pm, and the Holy Spirit met us in such a way that we didn't leave until midnight; bless my translator's heart he was a trooper! There was such a hunger and surrender, the harvest was ripe. One of my favorite stories is of a young man names Carlos who lived the street life and struggled with drug addiction. When he came up for prayer he said, "I don't even know how I am at church tonight, I've never been here and

I don't go to church." I told him that I prayed for him and just a few days before that and asked the Lord to bring those from the streets, those with drug addictions. I told him he was on God's mind and heart; he looked at me like "really, wow." I asked him if he wanted to receive Jesus as his Lord and Savior he said yes.

We led him in a prayer of salvation, and as his hands were raised, I encouraged him to begin to say to the Father, "Father I receive your love." As he did this I was praying for him, and sensed that he dealt with anger. I asked him if anger was an issue for him and he said, "yes even now I feel it rising." I placed my hand on his heart and commanded the spirit of anger to loose him. He literally broke out in a sweat and said that he felt heat through his body. He started to shake, and I asked him if he felt anger, and he said, "no" and started laughing with joy. I asked him if he felt like he wanted to speak in a language that he did not know, and he said, "yes" and was baptized in the Holy Spirit. This was uncontained freedom!

The Power of a Hug

There's a child, an elderly man or woman, a teenager out there waiting, yes waiting for a hug, not just any hug, but a hug from the Lord. A few days ago I had the privilege of meeting an awesome young woman of God. She is twenty-one years old, born and raised in El Salvador. She was part of a group we did ministry with, and she also assisted our team with translating. We were thrilled to have her spend a few nights with our team. One night before bed she wanted to talk with me. As we began to talk, she poured her heart out; she was broken and wounded due to a lack of relationship with her mother. They haven't seen each other in years and she has taken on a lot of responsibilities in her home.

I felt the Lord gently telling me to hug her like a mother would, and let her know it's not her fault that her mother left. She began crying as I told her how special she is and how much God loves her. I then asked her if I could hug her like a mother would, and I told her to come and sit on my lap and I held her like she was a little girl. She wept as I held her and prayed over her. When she got up, she said, "I know that hug was from God, I've only had one other hug like that in my life; I will never forget that hug because there is now peace in my heart." I looked at her face, and her whole countenance looked lighter. If God had me cross her path just so that He could hug her through me, it was absolutely worth it...that hug set her free!

Holy Spirit Come

We were in Bulgaria visiting one of the teams, the town that we were in felt so dry and dead. The pastor asked me to minister that Sunday, and I knew that the Holy Spirit wanted to pour out. I pressed into the Father's heart, and as the service started though the room was full of people, it felt so empty, void of presence. As they began to sing, the Holy Spirit began to speak to me about the fear that was holding people in bondage. I went up and started preaching and the power of the Holy Spirit began to flood the room! After service, the pastor told me that was the first time their church had ever experienced the power of the Holy Spirit. I'm so thankful He breathes the life of His Spirit into dead and dry places to bring resurrection.

Jericho Walls Fall

The afterschool program was supposed to start in three days, and though I had met with the school principal and given teachers registration forms for students, I didn't have one student signed up! I had a building, a program plan, but no students. I reminded the Lord that He sent me to Cayman Islands, and He reminded me that I am to walk by faith and not by sight. He then gave me the weirdest instruction He impressed it on my heart to walk through a whole afternoon plan as if I had a student in every chair, so I did, it was awkward at first, but within a few minutes I could see what I could not see.

Afterwards, I felt impressed to walk around the building seven times, and on the seventh time, I was to let out a shout so the Jericho walls would fall. I was okay with that except the building was right beside a very active health clinic so people would see me and hear me. In that moment, I had a choice to try and be cute or lose sight of my reputation for God to break forth with His plan and purpose. I chose the latter! That weekend I spent much time in prayer, and on the first day of school, I had a program full of children! Not only that, but the Lord opened the door for me to speak at three schools, and over three hundred kids received Jesus as their Lord and Savior, indeed the walls came down.

No Weapon Formed

We were in Uganda, and I told one of the girls on the team I was visiting that it felt like my right lung had been deflated. Within a day of sharing that I was struggling to breathe, I felt like I got hit by a truck. I went to the doctor, and he said, "have you ever heard of pneumonia this is what you have," he said my breathing was like that of an old woman with lung problems. They prescribed me medicine I started taking it, but began feeling worse. One of the nurses on the team slept right below me so that she could hear me if I needed anything.

I woke up in the middle of the night literally feeling like knives were stabbing me all over my body we took my temperature, and it was 104.6. We immediately went to the private hospital, the doctor explained that what I had been taking was not working and my blood cells counts looked a lot worse. He wrote a prescription for another medicine but warned that it was imported from Europe and may not be in stock. I went to the pharmacy the next day to learn that it wasn't in stock. I had prayer warriors bombarding heaven on my behalf. One of the girls had a Z-pak which is good for bronchitis; I felt the Lord's peace about taking it.

I was playing worship music and meditating on the Word of God continually. The pastor we were staying with came into the room one day full of zeal and said, "The Lord said the enemy is trying to take you out, but he cannot." In the midst of this, I still continued to check in with the team leaders and provide them with what they needed, whether wisdom, prayer, encouragement, or a listening ear. They would come to the bottom of my bed and sit while I laid there engaged in our time together. I believed the report of the Lord and continued with daily life acting on that belief. Within a few weeks, I celebrated my birthday with what felt like a new set of lungs.

Let Freedom Ring

So I arrived in Nairobi, Kenya on July 2nd. I kept thinking to myself "we are in Africa," it was a bit of a surreal moment. Over the next few days, we had incredible hospitality, food, and fellowship. On the night of July 3rd, our hostel owner took the leaders to a crusade that was going on in the slums, so that we could see what it was like. When we arrived, there was music playing, and people filled the street. The four of us were asked to come up and greet the people, so we did.

After everyone introduced themselves, I felt very strongly that I was supposed to pray for the people, and I was given permission to do so. After I prayed, I knew that the Lord was going to do something very special in the crusade. As we were about to leave, Pastor Angeline asked me to preach the next night at the crusade. I agreed to do so and knew that the Lord had something planned. We got to the crusade on July 4th, and noticed that the theme was resurrection and restoration, which was the icing on the cake. Our squad had a night of worship and intercession for Africa before arriving and its theme was reconciliation and restoration for Africa. I had an overwhelming expectation for God to show up big.

The crusade opened up with AMAZING praise and worship; I've never had so much fun dancing before the Lord. As praise and worship came to an end I was called up to the stage, as I took a deep breath and walked up I was more assured than ever that I was born for this, I was born to release the kingdom of heaven on earth. As I engaged with the people, the atmosphere became charged with excitement and expectation; and the Holy Spirit began to move as I preached on the life of Mary Magdeline. The power of God fell heavily, and women were freed from the bondage of shame prostitution branded on them, women were saved, and delivered from witchcraft. That indeed was the best 4th of July ever...a day we celebrated eternal freedom!!

As the Deer Pants for the Water

I spent the last month in Harbin, China with a team. While with the team, we would facilitate English corners at a local university, several students would attend, and this gave us an opportunity to connect with them as they practiced English with us. We began to build relationship with one of the sweet girls that we met during the English corner. One day, she was at our apartment, and she was so inspired by our stories to leave it all to travel around the world sharing the gospel of Jesus Christ. She shared her heart's desire to teach abroad. She shared that she didn't want to stay in China; however, to go against your parents' wishes, especially concerning education, was considered highly dishonoring. She wanted to record our stories and share them with her parents.

I remember her sharing that she would know that God is real if they give her permission to go abroad. Soon after that, she was given permission by her parents. We started a small Bible study group with her and a few other students. One of the girls from the team purchased a Bible for her. One of the songs that we sang was "As the Deer" and she loved it. At this point, she was curious to know more about Jesus, but not to surrender her life to Him yet. As the month came to an end and we were saying goodbye, I took her Skype information so that we could keep in touch. Maybe a month or so after I had returned to the United States I reached out to her, and she had been reading her Bible and wanted to receive Jesus as her personal Savior. I led her in a prayer of salvation, and we sang "As the Deer". From time to time I speak with her, and she is doing well.

Women at the Well

I was preparing to minister from John 4 at our women's retreat. It had been such a beautiful time already, and the weather in Antigua was perfect! One of my teammates was going to translate for me, and we had already preplanned it as I didn't feel adequate to preach a message in Spanish yet. It's funny how what we think we aren't ready for the Lord totally knows we are ready for. I had this overwhelming impression in my heart that the Holy Spirit was going to give me the words to preach the message without a translator. So I went and told my teammate what I was sensing from the Lord, and she said, "yep, I already know," it was total confirmation. When the time came for me to preach, I said to myself, "okay Holy Spirit, you got this." The word came forth with power, and at the end of the message, women were saved! Jesus had each of those women on His mind, and He made sure I had exactly what I needed so that He could meet their need for a Savior who gives living water that quenches thirst, as He is the well that never runs dry.

Your Days Were Written

It was one of my last days at the labor and delivery ward in Uganda. As you come into the delivery room, there is a bucket with dead babies to the left. Each woman had to see this image as she was preparing to birth her baby. We had experienced seeing a baby born with no skull, the mother was told early on in the pregnancy that something was wrong with the baby, but she didn't know exactly what it was. The baby only lived for a few minutes once she delivered, I can't imagine the sorrow that she felt.

This day we had a few women in the delivery room, one of them gave birth to a baby that was blue and not breathing. The doctor tried the standard medical procedures and as he was attempting to bring life to this baby, I saw what seemed like a snapshot of this precious life. In my heart I said, "no, this baby is not supposed to die, not this one." The gift of faith overwhelmed me, and after the doctor tried all that he knew to do, I asked if he could move over so I could pray. I laid my hands on the baby and said, "in Jesus name you shall live and not die, live in Jesus name." I moved back, and within moments, we heard the most beautiful cry.

"all the days ordained for you were written in His book before one of them came to be" Psalm 139:16 NIV

Epilogue

I believe that this book has taken you further and deeper into the Father's love and the discovery of your identity in Christ Jesus. Restoration of our soul is a continual journey that escorts us into becoming all we were created to be. We all have a divine love story that is worth living out loud, and sharing with others. With all the voices and sounds coming forth in the world right now, there has never been a more necessary time to raise the voice and sound of heaven's love and restoration. I would love to continue to journey with you so let's stay connected, visit my website **www.restoredmovement.net** to find out how!

Index

Endnotes

Chapter 2

1 "Bittachon" www.hebrew4christians.com

2 *Merriam-Webster Dictionary*, s.v. "Clutter."

3 "Brain Mapping" https://study.com/academy/lesson/what-is-brain-mapping-test-techniques.html

4 Ibid., s.v. "Cast Out."

5 Ibid., s.v. "Strive."

6 Ibid., s.v. "Acceptance."

7 *Cambridge Dictionary*, s.v "Abandonment."

8 *Collins English Dictionary*, s.v "Bandage."

9 Ibid., s.v. "Independence."

10 *Lexio*, s.v. "Lordship.", https://www.lexico.com

Chapter 4

11 *King James Bible Dictionary*, s.v. "Reconcile."

12 International Standard Bible Encyclopedia, s.v. "Ambassador."

About the Author

Kellie is a woman after God's own heart who is motivated by love, driven by faith, and abounding in grace. With a professional background in social work and counseling she has a passion to see individuals, families, communities, and nations restored to God's original design. Her own journey awakened compassion within her to respond to the call to walk with women from various nations, generations, and backgrounds on their journey of restoration, to become all that God has created them to be. Through mission work, Kellie has poured into the lives of women in Guatemala, Belize, Kenya, Bulgaria, Honduras, Uganda, China, Albania, Grand Cayman Island, El Salvador, Romania, Rwanda and Egypt. Also, she has spoken at women's conferences in New Jersey, New York, and Kentucky.

Made in the USA
Middletown, DE
30 September 2020